a to Z
Food

Beverley Mathias
and
Ruth Thomson

Illustrations: Stephen Iliffe

Franklin Watts
London/New York/Sydney/Toronto

© 1988 Franklin Watts
12a Golden Square
London W1

Franklin Watts Australia
14 Mars Road
Lane Cove
N.S.W. 2066

Franklin Watts Inc
387 Park Avenue South
New York, NY 10016

ISBN: 086313 783 0

Editor: Ruth Thomson
Design: Edward Kinsey

The authors, illustrator and
Publisher would like to thank the
staff of the Frank Barnes School for
their great help in the preparation
of the Signed English illustrations.

Photographs: Chris Fairclough

Illustrations © Stephen Iliffe

Typesetting: Lineage, Watford
Printed in Italy
by *Arti Grafiche* V. Bona S.p.A. - Torino

About this book

* This book has been designed for use by all people learning to read. It is both an information book and a reading book.

* The alphabet is used to provide a natural framework for the exploration of the book's topic and for language development.

* The simple sentences place the key words in context and extend appreciation of the subject.

* The superb photographs have been carefully selected to stimulate interest and discussion.

* The activities that conclude the book are designed to reinforce understanding and to encourage further involvement in the topic.

* A special feature of the book is the provision of Signed English and the Finger Spelling Alphabet for non-hearing readers. This feature is also intended to provide a fascinating introduction to sign language for all readers, teachers and parents.

Beverley Mathias
Ruth Thomson

Aa

Apples are hard and crunchy.

Apples   are   hard   and   crunchy.

Bb

The baker has made some **bread.**

| The | baker | has | made | some | bread. |

Cc

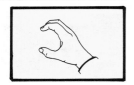

This **cake** has seven candles.

This   cake   has   seven   candles.

Dd

A hot drink warms you up.

A   hot   drink   warms   you   up.

Ee

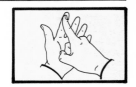

I like cracking boiled eggs.

| I | like | cracking | boiled | eggs. |

Ff

Which **fruit** do you like best?

Which   fruit   do   you   like   best?

Gg

Grapefruit tastes sour.

Grapefruit   tastes   sour.

Hh

Hamburgers are good to eat.

Hamburgers   are   good   to   eat.

Ice cream cools you down.

Ice cream   cools   you   down.

Jj

Juice is made from oranges.

Juice   is   made   from   oranges.

Kk

I like **ketchup** on my chips.

I   like   ketchup   on   my   chips.

Ll

Lettuce are grown in rows.

  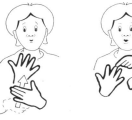 

Lettuce   are   grown   in   rows.

Mm

Mushrooms grow in the dark.

Mushrooms   grow   in   the   dark.

Nn

Nuts are hard to crack.

Nuts   are   hard   to   crack.

Onions make your eyes water.

Onions make your eyes water.

Pp

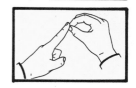

Potato skins are good for you.

Potato

skins

are

good

for

you.

 **Qq**

People queue to buy food.

People   queue   to   buy   food.

Rr

I eat **rice** with chopsticks.

I   eat   rice   with   chopsticks.

Ss

We like **sandwiches** for lunch.

We   like   sandwiches   for   lunch.

Tt

Do you like **toast** for breakfast?

Do   you   like   toast   for   breakfast?

Uu

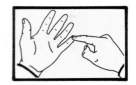

Carrots grow underground.

Carrots   grow   underground.

Vv

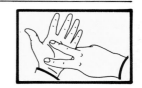

Vegetables have different shapes.

Vegetables   have   different   shapes.

Ww

Iced **water** is very cold.

Iced　　　　water　　　　is　　　　very　　　　cold.

Xx

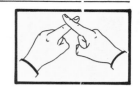

Six eggs fit in each box.

Six   eggs   fit   in   each   box.

Yy

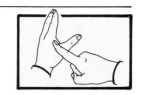

Yogurt is made from milk.

Yogurt   is   made   from   milk.

Zz

Pumpkins can be any size!

| Pumpkins | can | be | any | size! |

What foods do you like?

We need food to help us grow, to give us energy and to keep us healthy.

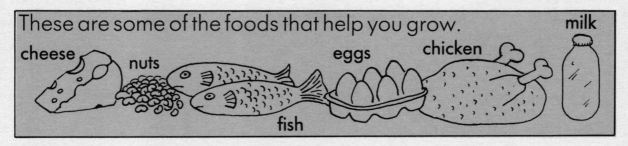

These are some of the foods that help you grow.

cheese nuts milk eggs chicken fish

These are some of the foods that give you energy.

bread rice cake potatoes noodles cereal

These are some of the foods that help keep you healthy.

fruit and vegetables

Think of some other foods you like and see if you know which of these groups they belong to.

Draw three plates of food that you might eat in one day. Also draw any snacks you have between meals.

breakfast **lunch/dinner** **tea** **snacks**

Now make a chart like this one and write in all the foods on your plates. Colour the words to show what sort of food they are. For example if you had cereal and milk for breakfast, then colour the word cereal yellow (an energy food) and the milk blue (a growing food).

○ Growing food   ○ Energy food   ○ Food which keeps you healthy

breakfast
Cereal Milk

lunch/dinner

tea

snacks

Do you eat some of each sort of food? Which sort of food do you eat most of?

I went to market (a game for two or more people)

Play this game, either saying or signing the name of foods.

The first player starts by saying, 'I went to market and I bought an apple,' or any other food beginning with a. The second player says, 'I went to market and I bought an apple and a banana' or any other food beginning with b. The next player repeats the shopping list and adds a food beginning with c, and so on through the alphabet. If a player can't remember the list or gets one wrong, he loses a life.

A player who loses three lives is out of the game.

The Finger Spelling Alphabet

A
B
C
D
E
F
G
H
I
J
K
L
M
N
O
P
Q
R
S
T
U
V
W
X
Y
Z